M000287204

For the Teacher

This reproducible study guide to use in conjunction with the novel *From the Mixed-up Files of Mrs. Basil E. Frankweiler* consists of lessons for guided reading. Written in chapter-by-chapter format, the guide contains a synopsis, pre-reading activities, vocabulary and comprehension exercises, as well as extension activities to be used as follow-up to the novel.

In a homogeneous classroom, whole class instruction with one title is appropriate. In a heterogeneous classroom, reading groups should be formed: each group works on a different novel at its own reading level. Depending upon the length of time devoted to reading in the classroom, each novel, with its guide and accompanying lessons, may be completed in three to six weeks.

Begin using NOVEL-TIES for reading development by distributing the novel and a folder to each child. Distribute duplicated pages of the study guide for students to place in their folders. After examining the cover and glancing through the book, students can participate in several pre-reading activities. Vocabulary questions should be considered prior to reading a chapter; all other work should be done after the chapter has been read. Comprehension questions can be answered orally or in writing. The classroom teacher should determine the amount of work to be assigned, always keeping in mind that readers must be nurtured and that the ultimate goal is encouraging students' love of reading.

The benefits of using NOVEL-TIES are numerous. Students read good literature in the original, rather than in abridged or edited form. The good reading habits, formed by practice in focusing on interpretive comprehension and literary techniques, will be transferred to the books students read independently. Passive readers become active, avid readers.

Novel-Ties® are printed on recycled paper.

SYNOPSIS

Sixth-grader Claudia Kincaid is bored and dissatisfied with her life in Greenwich, Connecticut. Feeling unappreciated by her parents and seeking relief from the routine of chores and school, she decides to run away to the Metropolitan Museum of Art in New York City. She chooses her brother Jamie as her companion, mainly because he has a talent for managing money.

Claudia loves the elegance and beauty of the Museum; both children are enchanted with the exhibits the Museum has to offer. They become particularly interested in a statue of an angel, which the Museum had purchased from the collection of Mrs. Basil E. Frankweiler for $225. They are intrigued by the possibility that the statue may be the work of the famous Renaissance artist Michelangelo.

Claudia and Jamie must use their wits just to keep themselves hidden from the museum employees as they decide to tackle the mystery of the angel. After researching Michelangelo at the public library, Claudia and Jamie return to the Museum and examine the statue again. They find what they believe to be the artist's mark on the underside of the statue. They write to the museum officials hoping that by identifying the statue as Michelangelo's work, they will be recognized as heroes by the Museum. The Museum, however, does not believe that this solves the mystery because someone other than Michelangelo could have carved this mark.

In a final attempt to solve the mystery, Claudia and Jamie visit Mrs. Frankweiler. She strikes a bargain with the children: if they tell her all about their adventure, she will allow them to search her files for information about the statue.

After a frantic search in Mrs. Frankweiler's filing cabinets, Claudia and Jamie find sketches by Michelangelo which seem to prove that he was the artist who carved the sculpture. Complying with Mrs. Frankweiler's wishes, they all agree not to tell anyone about the sketches. Claudia and Jamie return home, excited by their adventures and changed by their secret discovery. Mrs. Frankweiler decides to leave the sketches to the Kincaid children in her will. Claudia and Jamie will be able to decide what to do with their secret when they are older.

BACKGROUND INFORMATION

Michelangelo

Michelangelo Buonarroti was born on March 6, 1475 in Caprese, Italy. When he was thirteen, his parents reluctantly apprenticed him to Domenico Ghirlandaio, who at the time was painting a chapel in the church of Santa Maria Novella in Florence. Here, Michelangelo learned the technique of fresco (painting on fresh plaster before it dries); a technique he would use many years later in the Sistine Chapel in Rome. When he was fifteen, Michelangelo began to spend time in the home of Lorenzo de' Medici, where he studied sculpture under Bertoldo di Giovanni. During this time, he completed the *Madonna of the Stairs* and the *Battle of the Centaurs*. After Lorenzo de' Medici died Michelangelo left Florence, going first to Bologna and then to Rome. In Rome, he carved the *Bacchus* and then the *Pietà* which is in St. Peter's basilica in Rome.

In 1501, Michelangelo returned to Florence where he began work on the *David*. This statue was completed in 1504. During this same period, Michelangelo produced several Madonnas; including the painting the *Holy Family* (also known as the *Doni Madonna*), a statue of the *Madonna and Child* (called the *Bruges Madonna*), and two marble reliefs, the *Taddei tondo* and the *Pitti tondo*.

In 1508, Michelangelo began work on his most important project, the Sistine Chapel ceiling frescoes, a task that would occupy him until 1512. Upon completing the Sistine Chapel, Michelangelo was regarded as the greatest living artist. In 1513, Michelangelo returned to Florence to complete the facade of San Lorenzo, work for Pope Leo X, the Medici family's church and designed the Laurentian library.

In 1534, Michelangelo left Florence for Rome, where he spent the remainder of his life. He returned to the Sistine Chapel where he created the *Last Judgment*, another fresco, on the end wall. He designed the dome for St. Peter's and the Capitoline Square. He also worked on the Palazzo Farnese. His last paintings were the frescoes of the *Conversion of St. Paul* and the *Crucifixion of St. Peter* in the Pauline Chapel in the Vatican. Michelangelo died on February 18, 1564.

PRE-READING ACTIVITIES

1. Preview the book by reading the title and the author's name and by looking at the illustration on the cover. What do you think the book will be about? Where does it take place? Have you read anything else by the same author?

2. Read the Background Information and do some additional research to learn about the artist Michelangelo. Then fill in the first two columns of a K-W-L chart such as the one below. When you finish the book, return to the chart to complete column three.

Michelangelo

What I Know –K–	What I Would Like To Learn –W–	What I Learned –L–

3. **Art Connection:** Locate a book that shows the sketches and sculptures of the Italian Renaissance artist Michelangelo. Study these pictures to determine why this artist's works have been treasured for centuries.

4. **Cooperative Learning Activity:** Work with a small group of your classmates to discuss the basic elements of survival: food, shelter, and clothing. Then consider these additional elements: companionship, protection, money, and recreation. Compare the importance of these elements in the following kinds of environments:
   • tropical island
   • metropolitan city
   • rural wilderness
   • desert
   As you read the book, consider how the children survived in their environment.

5. Have you ever wanted to run away from home? If so, why did you want to leave? How long did you stay away? Why did you return? If you were now to choose to live independently for several weeks, where might be the best place? What would be your survival plan should you stay in this place?

6. Ask nearby museums for their floor plans and descriptive literature. You may also write to several museums for this information. Examine them carefully. Think about the different kinds of museums that exist and the various functions of museums. What have been your museum experiences?

7. What role do communications media (such as the Internet, television, radio, and newspapers) play in finding lost children? How can publicity help in finding missing children? Can widespread news coverage ever hinder police investigations?

Pre-Reading Activities (cont.)

8. What is the job of a museum curator? Invite a museum curator to your school. Prepare a list of questions that you would like to ask this person.

9. Have you ever been told a secret that had to remain private for a long time? If you had a secret to share, whom would you entrust with the information? Do you like to know a secret or do you feel it is a burden?

> **Note:** The floor plans of the Metropolitan Museum of Art in New York City, shown in Chapter Four, reflect the museum's actual floor plan as it existed in 1967, when this book was written. Although many objects remain in the same place, you would notice some changes and additions if you were to visit today.

INTRODUCTION, CHAPTERS 1, 2

Vocabulary: Use the definition of the first underlined word in each of the following sentences to help you figure out the meaning of the second underlined word.

1. If something that is <u>monotonous</u> never changes, describe the voice of a <u>monotone</u>.

   _____

   _____

2. If <u>muffling</u> a sound makes it softer, what is the purpose of a <u>muffler</u> on a car?

   _____

   _____

3. If a <u>decision</u> is a definite choice or opinion, how would you describe a <u>decisive</u> tone of voice.

   _____

   _____

4. If you plan carefully when you <u>calculate</u> your next move in a game, how would you describe a <u>calculating</u> person?

   _____

   _____

5. If to <u>commute</u> means to travel regularly between one's home and workplace, then who is a <u>commuter</u>?

   _____

   _____

6. If an <u>urban</u> area is a city, where are the <u>suburbs</u>?

   _____

   _____

7. If <u>company</u> means a group of people gathered together for social purposes, then what kind of person would you choose as your <u>companion</u> for an evening at the movies?

   _____

   _____

8. If to <u>postpone</u> means to put off to a later date, then what would a notice saying "Concert <u>Postponement</u>" suggest?

   _____

   _____

Introduction, Chapters 1, 2 (cont.)

> Read to learn about Claudia and Jamie's destination.

Questions:

1. Why did the novel begin with Mrs. Frankweiler's letter to her lawyer?

2. What were the main reasons that Claudia ran away from home?

3. Why did Claudia choose the Metropolitan Museum of Art as her destination?

4. Why did Claudia want her brother Jamie to go with her? Why did he agree to go with her?

5. Why was Claudia able to activate her plan sooner than she expected?

6. What was Jamie's first reaction when he learned that they would be going to the Metropolitan Museum of Art? What changed his attitude?

7. How did Claudia and Jamie get to New York City from their home in Greenwich, Connecticut?

Questions for Discussion:

1. Do you think Claudia had good reasons to want to run away? Do you think her brother had good reasons to join her? Could she have solved her problem any other way?

2. Claudia left her mother and father a note telling them not to worry or call the FBI because she and Jamie were leaving home. Do you think their parents will receive the note calmly? What do you think they will do when they receive it?

3. What do you think Mrs. Frankweiler meant when she wrote, "Manhattan called for the courage of at least two Kincaids"?

Literary Element: Characterization

The novel begins with a short letter written by Mrs. Basil E. Frankweiler to her lawyer. What words in the letter suggest that she is . . .

wealthy _____

elderly _____

intelligent _____

What other words would you use to describe her, based upon the language in this letter?

_____

_____

_____

Introduction, Chapters 1, 2 (cont.)

Literary Devices:

I. *Point of View*—Point of view refers to the voice telling the story: it could be the author or one of the characters in the book. From whose point of view is this story told?

    _____

    How might this story have changed if told from Claudia's mother's point of view?

    _____

    _____

    _____

II. *Simile*—A simile is a figure of speech in which a comparison between two unlike objects is stated directly using the words "like" or "as." For example:

        The bus bounced along like an empty cracker box on wheels—
        almost empty.

    What is being compared?

    _____

    Why is this an apt comparison?

    _____

    _____

Writing Activity:

When Claudia was riding on the bus on the first leg of the adventure, she said that her heart sounded "like their electric percolator brewing the morning's coffee." Describe a time when you could feel your heart pounding with excitement or fear.

CHAPTERS 3, 4

Vocabulary: Use the context to figure out the meaning of the underlined word in each of the following sentences. Then compare your definition with one you find in a dictionary.

1. The silk and wool <u>tapestry</u> hanging on the west wall portrayed a handsome king and his knights.

   Your definition_____

   Dictionary definition _____

2. If you visit Paris, be sure to see the <u>sarcophagus</u> in which Napoleon is entombed.

   Your definition_____

   Dictionary definition _____

3. The <u>curator</u> of modern paintings decided that the works of Picasso should be displayed in the museum's second floor gallery.

   Your definition_____

   Dictionary definition _____

4. The experts agreed that the painting was a <u>masterpiece</u>.

   Your definition_____

   Dictionary definition _____

5. The <u>sculptor</u> put the finishing touches on the marble statue.

   Your definition_____

   Dictionary definition _____

6. The Greeks used designs from everyday life and from myth to decorate their <u>urns</u>.

   Your definition_____

   Dictionary definition _____

> Read to find out what it is like to hide out in an art museum.

Questions:

1. How did Jamie prove his ability as treasurer?
2. What precautions did the children take so they would not be noticed by the guards at the museum?
3. On what two occasions did Jamie forget the "inconspicuous" rule?
4. Why did Jamie change his mind about sleeping on the bed with the canopy?

Chapters 3, 4 (cont.)

5. How did Claudia and Jamie's relationship change as they began living together as runaways?

6. How did Claudia think she and her brother should spend their time while they were hiding out in the museum?

7. Why did the statue of the angel draw such large crowds? Why did the museum suggest that this statue had been a great bargain?

8. Why did the children decide to concentrate on learning about the statue?

Questions for Discussion:

1. Look at the floor plans for the Metropolitan Museum in Chapter Four. If you were living at the museum, what two areas would you want to study first? What would you want to find out?

2. What do you think would happen if the guards discovered the children?

Literary Device: Simile

What is being compared in the following simile?

> Their [Claudia's and Jamie's] stomachs felt like tubes of toothpaste that had been all squeezed out.

_____

Why is this better than saying, "Claudia and Jamie were very hungry."

_____

_____

_____

Math Connection:

Start a balance sheet showing how much money the children had when they began their adventure and what they spent along the way. You will have to estimate some of the costs and remember that items would be much cheaper because the book was written in 1967.

Writing Activity:

Claudia chose her brother Jamie as a companion on this adventure because she believed that his personality balanced her own. Write about one person you know who would be good company on a similar adventure. Tell about this person's personality, how you are alike, how you are different, and about any adventures you may have had together.

SPECIAL ACTIVITY: SURVIVAL

Survival for Claudia and Jamie required careful planning and problem-solving. Use the chart below to describe how they solved each of these problems.

Problem	Solution
Obtaining Food	
Finding a Sleeping Place	
Keeping Clean	
Avoiding Notice	

CHAPTERS 5, 6

Vocabulary: Synonyms are words with similar meanings. Draw a line from each word in column A to its synonym in column B. Then use the numbered words in column A to fill in the blanks in the sentences below.

A	B
1. dismal	a. expert
2. vendor	b. beating
3. authority	c. feelings
4. stealthy	d. gloomy
5. throbbing	e. seriously
6. humility	f. sneaky
7. sternly	g. modesty
8. emotions	h. seller

. . . .

1. Because the burglar was so _____ and clever, the police had difficulty capturing him.

2. The judge spoke _____ as he pronounced a verdict of guilty.

3. After the race, her heart seemed to be _____ a mile a minute.

4. We tried to cheer up the bare, _____ room with a coat of yellow paint.

5. The buyer was trying to convince the _____ to lower the price.

6. It was silly to ask a beginning student when a(n) _____ is easily available.

7. He tried to control his _____ so no one would see that he was about to cry.

8. Her _____ would not allow her to brag about her achievements.

> Read to find out why Claudia and Jamie become fascinated with a piece of sculpture.

Questions:

1. In what ways did Claudia insist that her life in the museum be like life at home?

2. What part of the research task on Michelangelo did Claudia assign to Jamie? Why was this an appropriate assignment?

3. What was the significance of the "crushed up" mark on the velvet near the statue? Who did Claudia and Jamie want to tell about their discovery?

Chapters 5, 6 (cont.)

4. Why wasn't Claudia ready to return home?

5. What was the double meaning of Jamie's pun at the end of Chapter Six, "they should try to get to the *bottom* of the mystery"?

Questions for Discussion:

1. Why do you think Claudia and Jamie didn't experience homesickness?

2. Do you think Claudia and Jamie should use the coins in the fountain?

3. Do you think the children will be able to solve the mystery?

Events in Sequence: Number the following events in the order they have taken place in the story so far.

_____ They avoided the guards at closing time and slept in an ancient bed.

_____ They decided to do some research on Michelangelo to find clues about the origin of the angel statue.

_____ All they had to do now was to convince the Museum authorities.

_____ Claudia and Jamie left their home in Greenwich, Connecticut.

_____ The mark they found on the bottom of the statue matched the mark they found in their research.

_____ Claudia and Jamie become very interested in an angel statue that may have been sculpted by Michelangelo.

_____ Their destination was the Metropolitan Museum of Art in New York City.

Writing Activity:

What do you think the museum director would do with the evidence the Kincaid children gave to him in their letter? Write the letter he might have written in response. After you read Chapter Eight, compare your letter to the one the children actually received.

> **Note:** The fountain in the restaurant at the Metropolitan Museum of Art that was described in Chapter Five no longer exists. This was a controversial change: many people thought the pool with its fountain and statues were an artistic landmark.

Chapters 5, 6 (cont.)

Literary Element: Characterization

Some of the adjectives below might be used to describe either Claudia or Jamie. Other words will fit both children. Place a check [✓] in the appropriate column next to each adjective. Leave a blank next to words that do not fit either child. Add some adjectives of your own to the list.

Adjective	Claudia	Jamie
1. daring		
2. homesick		
3. frugal		
4. inquisitive		
5. resourceful		
6. gloomy		
7. cooperative		
8. clever		
9. bossy		
10. remorseful		
11.		
12.		
13.		
14.		
15.		

CHAPTERS 7, 8

Vocabulary: Antonyms are words with opposite meanings. Draw a line from each word in column A to its antonym in column B. Then use the words in column A to fill in the blanks in the sentences below.

	A			B	
1.	scowl		a.	genuine	
2.	solemn		b.	race	
3.	counterfeit		c.	retain	
4.	reject		d.	smile	
5.	risky		e.	withdraw	
6.	approach		f.	joyous	
7.	stroll		g.	safe	

· ·

1. The computer will _____ any answer that is incorrect and ask you to try again.

2. As soon as we saw her _____ expression, we knew that she had failed the test.

3. Red lights will begin to flash at the _____ of a train.

4. The stunt driver never worried about her _____ occupation.

5. Try not to _____ when the photographer is ready to take your picture.

6. It is pleasant to _____ in the park on a cool sunny day.

7. The thieves were trying to pass off _____ money as the real thing.

> Read to find out how the museum director responds to the children's letter.

Questions:

1. What did Claudia mean when she said, "We'll take a long, long bath tonight"?

2. Why wouldn't Claudia allow Jamie to speak to the students in the Egyptian tomb?

3. Why were Claudia and Jamie "disappointed beyond words" after they received a letter from Harold C. Lowery?

CHAPTERS 7, 8 (cont.)

4. Why didn't Claudia want to go home and forget about the angel?

5. Why did Jamie and Claudia go to Farmington, Connecticut?

Question for Discussion:

From what you know of Mrs. Frankweiler, do you think she will help Claudia and Jamie?

Social Studies Connection:

Jamie says that Claudia wants to be Joan of Arc, Clara Barton, and Florence Nightingale. Who were these famous women? Do some research to find out about each one.

Writing Activity:

Imagine that the children at the Egyptian tomb recognized Jamie. Write a short narrative or dialogue in which you express this possibility. What questions might the children ask Claudia and Jamie? Would Claudia and Jamie reveal their secret or make up an excuse for their presence?

CHAPTERS 9, 10

Vocabulary: In the sentences below, each of the underlined words has more than one meaning. Use the context of the sentence to help you decide which meaning fits. Write the letter of the correct definition on the line next to each sentence.

peers

    a) looks at closely

    b) people who are your equals

1. Because he wanted the approval of his <u>peers</u>, he followed them in their mischief.   _____

2. She <u>peers</u> at the small print because she cannot find her glasses.   _____

bargain

    a) something purchased at a low price

    b) agreement to do something in return for something else

3. Because it was the end of the season, the skis were a real <u>bargain</u>.   _____

4. If I don't keep my part of the <u>bargain</u>, you will never trust me again.   _____

dull

    a) not having a sharp edge or point; blunt

    b) boring

5. The <u>dull</u> performance put him to sleep.   _____

6. The knife was so <u>dull</u>, it could not even cut bread.   _____

will

    a) desire or wish

    b) legal statement giving the final settlement of a person's property after he or she dies.

7. The king's <u>will</u> became law automatically.   _____

8. After the funeral, they gathered to hear the reading of the <u>will</u>.   _____

filed

    a) lined up, one behind the other

    b) smoothed down, with a tool

9. They <u>filed</u> out of the room in an orderly manner.   _____

10. I <u>filed</u> my nail after it broke.   _____

CHAPTERS 9, 10

Vocabulary: In the sentences below, each of the underlined words has more than one meaning. Use the context of the sentence to help you decide which meaning fits. Write the letter of the correct definition on the line next to each sentence.

peers

    a) looks at closely

    b) people who are your equals

1. Because he wanted the approval of his <u>peers</u>, he followed them in their mischief.   _____

2. She <u>peers</u> at the small print because she cannot find her glasses.   _____

bargain

    a) something purchased at a low price

    b) agreement to do something in return for something else

3. Because it was the end of the season, the skis were a real <u>bargain</u>.   _____

4. If I don't keep my part of the <u>bargain</u>, you will never trust me again.   _____

dull

    a) not having a sharp edge or point; blunt

    b) boring

5. The <u>dull</u> performance put him to sleep.   _____

6. The knife was so <u>dull</u>, it could not even cut bread.   _____

will

    a) desire or wish

    b) legal statement giving the final settlement of a person's property after he or she dies.

7. The king's <u>will</u> became law automatically.   _____

8. After the funeral, they gathered to hear the reading of the <u>will</u>.   _____

filed

    a) lined up, one behind the other

    b) smoothed down, with a tool

9. They <u>filed</u> out of the room in an orderly manner.   _____

10. I <u>filed</u> my nail after it broke.   _____

Chapters 9, 10 (cont.)

Read to find out about the bargain Mrs. Frankweiler makes with Claudia and Jamie.

Questions:

1. How did Mrs. Frankweiler know that Claudia and Jamie were the missing children?

2. Why did Mrs. Frankweiler want to meet Claudia and Jamie?

3. Why was Claudia surprised that running away had caused such a commotion at home?

4. What was the bargain that Mrs. Frankweiler made with the children?

5. Where did Claudia and Jamie finally find the information about the angel?

6. Why did Mrs. Frankweiler want her proof about the angel statue to remain a secret?

7. Besides being Mrs. Frankweiler's lawyer, who was Saxonberg? Why did Mrs. Frankweiler tell him this story?

Questions for Discussion:

1. Do you think that the information in Mrs. Frankweiler's file proved that Michelangelo had sculpted the angel?

2. How do you know that the children have become fond of Mrs. Frankweiler?

Writing Activity:

Mrs. Basil E. Frankweiler defined happiness as "excitement that has found a settling down place, but there is always a little corner that keeps flapping around." Write about those things that have made you happy in the past and those things that you hope will happen to make you happy in the future. Use Mrs. Frankweiler's definition of happiness or develop your own.

CLOZE ACTIVITY

The following passage has been taken from Chapter Four of the novel. Read it through entirely and then use the context to fill in each blank with one word that makes sense. Afterwards, you may compare you language with that of the author.

On the second day the crowd going up the broad staircase to see the little Angel was even greater. The _____[1] article had made people curious. Besides, it _____[2] a cloudy day, and museum attendance always _____[3] in bad weather. Some people who had _____[4] been to the Metropolitan Museum for years _____[5] Some people who had never been there _____,[6] came; they got directions from maps, subway _____,[7] and police. (I'm surprised, Saxonberg, that seeing my _____[8] in the paper in connection with Michelangelo _____[9] bring even you to the museum. You _____[10] have profited more than you would have _____[11] by that trip. Are photo albums of _____[12] grandchildren the only pictures you look at? _____[13] you altogether unconscious of the magic of the _____[14] of Michelangelo? I truly believe that _____[15] name has magic even now; the best _____[16] of magic because it comes from true _____.[17] Claudia sensed it as she again stood _____[18] line. The mystery only intrigued her; the _____[19] trapped her.)

Both children were annoyed when _____[20] guards plus the push of the crowd _____[21] them past the Angel. How could they _____[22] look for fingerprints when they were so _____?[23] After this hurried visit to the statue, they _____[24] to do their research when they _____[25] the statue and the museum to _____.[26] Claudia especially wanted to make herself important _____[27] the statue. She would solve its mystery; and it, in turn, would do something important to her, though what this was, she didn't quite know.

POST-READING ACTIVITIES

1. Return to the K-W-L chart on Michelangelo that you began in the Pre-Reading Activities on page three of this study guide. Complete the third column and compare your responses with those of your classmates.

2. Return to the survival chart that you began on page ten of this study guide. Add more information and compare your responses with those of your classmates.

3. With your classmates, develop a survival chart, using the same problems that appear on the chart on page ten of this study guide, for survival in your school building.

4. Return to the characterization chart that you began on page thirteen of this study guide. Add more adjectives and compare your responses with those of your classmates.

5. If possible, take a field trip to an art museum in your area. Find several paintings or statues that appeal to you. Notice the artists' names, pertinent dates, and any text that may accompany the art. Then, after the museum trip, do some in-depth research at the library on the artists and the works of art you choose. If no art museum is available, a good illustrated textbook on art history or a virtual visit to a museum online may substitute.

6. If Claudia and Mrs. Frankweiler had not decided to keep their secret, the newspaper would surely have carried an article about this amazing discovery. Write a newspaper article about the angel statue, revealing the information about it that you found in the book.

7. Role-play the parts of Jamie and Claudia with a friend. Imagine that you are being interviewed for a television talk show after you return home from your adventure.

8. Although *The Mixed-up Files* is a fantasy and is written in a light-hearted tone, the issue of young runaways in cities and the dangers they face is extremely serious. Discuss the real-life situation that exists for runaways in metropolitan centers.

9. The setting of the book, the Metropolitan Museum of Art, is an important cultural institution in New York City that attracts millions of visitors each year. Select other places of interest that could be used as a setting for a story about runaways. You could then write a story or an outline for a story set in this new location.

10. Although the reader never meets Saxonberg, Mrs. Frankweiler makes comments addressed to him throughout the book. These comments reveal a great deal about Saxonberg and Mrs. Frankweiler's opinion of him. Write a description of Saxonberg, based upon Mrs. Frankweiler's remarks.

Post-Reading Activities (cont.)

11. The children are planning to visit Mrs. Frankweiler again. Write what you think might happen if they do revisit her.

12. **Fluency/Readers Theater:** Select a chapter from the book that has a lot of dialogue among several characters such as Chapter Four. Each character's dialogue should be read by one student. The characters should read only those words inside the quotation marks. Ignore phrases such as "he said" or "she said." One student can read the narration. Use simple props, such as hats, to identify the characters.

13. **Literature Circle:** Have a literature circle discussion in which you tell your personal reactions to *The Mixed-up Files of Mrs. Basil E. Frankweiler*. Here are some questions and sentence starters to help your literature circle begin a discussion.

    - How are you like Claudia and Jamie? How are you different?
    - Do you find the characters in the book realistic? Why or why not?
    - Which character did you like the most? The least?
    - Who else would like to read the book? Why?
    - What questions would you like to ask the author about this book?
    - I would have liked to see . . .
    - I wonder . . .
    - Claudia learned that . . .
    - Mrs. Frankweiler learned that . . .

SUGGESTIONS FOR FURTHER READING

Christian, Mary Blunt. *Sebastian and the Bone to Pick Mystery*. Simon & Schuster.

Corcoran, Barbara. *Cabin in the Sky*. Simon & Schuster.

* Cleary, Beverly. *Ramona the Brave*. HarperCollins.

* Fitzgerald, John. *The Great Brain*. Penguin.

* Fitzhugh, Louise. *Harriet the Spy*. Random House.

* George, Jean Craighead. *My Side of the Mountain*. Penguin.

* Holman, Felice. *Slake's Limbo*. Simon & Schuster.

Hunter, Kristin. *Lou in the Limelight*. Simon & Schuster.

Hildick. E. W. *The Secret Spenders*. Random House.

Lingard, Joan. *Snake Among the Sunflowers*. Penguin.

* Levoy, Myron. *The Witch of Fourth Street*. HarperCollins.

Mackellar, William. *The Kid Who Owned Manhattan Island*. Dodd, Mead.

* Merrill, Jean. *The Pushcart War*. Random House.

* Nelson, O.T. *The Girl Who Owned a City*. Random House.

* O'Dell, Scott. *Island of the Blue Dolphins*. Random House.

* Paulsen, Gary. *Hatchet*. Penguin.

* Seldon, George. *The Cricket in Times Square*. Random House.

Stolz, Mary. *The Noonday Friends*. HarperCollins.

* Taylor, Theodore. *The Cay*. HarperCollins.

Other Books by E. L. Konigsberg

About the B'nai Bagels. Simon & Schuster.

Altogether, One At a Time. Simon & Schuster.

Amy Elizabeth Explores Bloomingdales. Simon & Schuster.

The Dragon in the Ghetto Caper. Simon & Schuster.

Father's Arcane Daughter. Simon & Schuster.

* *Jennifer, Hecate, Macbeth, William McKinley and Me, Elizabeth*. Simon & Schuster.

Journey to an 800 Number. Simon & Schuster.

The Outcasts of 19 Schuyler Place. Simon & Schuster.

A Proud Taste of Scarlet and Miniver. Simon & Schuster.

Samuel Todd's Book of Great Colors. Simon & Schuster.

The Second Mrs. Giaconda. Simon & Schuster.

Silent to the Bone. Simon & Schuster.

T-backs, T-shirts, Coat and Suit. Simon & Schuster.

* *The View from Saturday*. Simon & Schuster.

* NOVEL-TIES study guides are available for these titles.

ANSWER KEY

Intro, Chapters 1, 2

Vocabulary: 1. The voice of a monotone is dull because every sound is on the same note. 2. The muffler on a car diminishes the sound of its engine. 3. A decisive tone of voice is one that reflects a strong opinion. 4. A calculating person plots and plans carefully for any action taken. 5. A commuter is someone who travels to and from his or her workplace each day. 6. The suburbs are the smaller towns and cities surrounding a major city. 7. A good companion is someone who is sociable and pleasant to be with. 8. "Concert Postponement" suggests that the concert will be put off to a later date.

Questions: 1. The letter established the fact that Mrs. Frankweiler was changing her will because of the reasons she was going to write about. The substance of this written explanation was the book that followed. 2. Claudia ran away from home because of her parents' injustice and her boredom with her daily routine. 3. Claudia chose the museum because it was beautiful and comfortable. 4. Claudia wanted Jamie to go with her because he was skilled at handling money and this skill would be important when they left home. He also could be counted on to be quiet and he was funny. Jamie agreed to go along because he succumbed to his sister's flattery. 5. Claudia was able to activate her plan sooner than expected because she found an unpunched train ticket in the wastebasket, which allowed her to stretch her very limited budget. 6. At first, Jamie was disappointed to learn that the museum was their destination. He assumed they would be hiding in the woods. His attitude changed after Claudia convinced him there would be adventure and he could be treasurer. 7. Claudia and Jamie hid on the school bus and then took the train, using the ticket Claudia had found in the wastebasket.

Chapters 3, 4

Vocabulary: 1. tapestry–cloth with pictures woven into it 2. sarcophagus–stone coffin 3. curator–person in charge of the collections of a museum 4. masterpiece–great work of art 5. sculptor–artist who creates a statue or artwork in three dimensions 6. urns–vases

Questions: 1. Jamie showed that he was a good treasurer by carefully watching their money: he insisted that he and Claudia walk to the museum, rather than spend money on a taxi as his sister demanded; and he chose to eat in the cafeteria because it was cheaper than the restaurant. 2. To avoid the guards, Claudia and Jamie re-entered the museum by the back door and hid in the washrooms until the guards left their posts. 3. Forgetting the "inconspicuous" rule, Jamie almost allowed his picture to be taken, and he asked a question while accompanying a class tour. 4. Jamie changed his mind about the bed because he was intrigued that someone had been murdered in it. 5. Claudia and Jamie started to work as a team, really caring for one another. 6. Claudia thought that she and her brother should learn everything about the museum, one thing at a time. 7. The statue drew large crowds because it was suspected that the angel was the work of Michelangelo, even though the museum had purchased it for only $225. 8. Claudia and Jamie wanted to solve the mystery of the statue to find out whether Michelangelo was really its creator.

Chapters 5, 6

Vocabulary: 1. d 2. h 3. a 4. f 5. b 6. g 7. e 8. c; 1. stealthy 2. sternly 3. throbbing 4. dismal 5. vendor 6. authority 7. emotions 8. humility

Questions: 1. So that living in the museum could be similar to life at home, Claudia insisted that she and Jamie sleep in a bed, change underwear daily, bathe, launder clothes, and eat regular meals. 2. Claudia had Jamie look at Michelangelo's pictures while she researched the writings. She was able to read and comprehend with greater proficiency than her brother. 3. The mark had been made on the velvet when the statue was resting on it. The children suspected that the "M" with the three circles was Michelangelo's mark. This might prove its authenticity. They wanted to tell the museum director about their discovery. 4. Claudia didn't want to return home until she had become a different person with the secret of the statue belonging just to her. 5. The expression commonly means to solve a mystery. In this case it also refers to the base of the statue which may have the clue to solve the mystery.

Events in Sequence: 3, 5, 7, 1, 6, 4, 2

Chapters 7, 8

Vocabulary: 1. d 2. f 3. a 4. c 5. g 6. e 7. b; 1. reject 2. solemn 3. approach 4. risky 5. scowl 6. stroll 7. counterfeit

Questions: 1. Claudia meant that she and her brother would collect enough coins from the bottom of the museum fountain to be able to afford the post office box. 2. Claudia wouldn't allow Jamie to talk to the students in the Egyptian tomb because they were the students in Jamie's third-grade class, and she didn't want to be recognized. 3. The letter was a disappointment because it said that the museum was waiting for more expert opinions on the statue's origins and they did not feel Claudia and Jamie's evidence was sufficient. 4. Claudia didn't want to go home until she had a secret that would make her feel different and special. 5. Claudia and Jamie went to visit Mrs. Frankweiler at her home in Farmington, Connecticut, hoping that she might provide more clues to the angel statue.

Chapters 9, 10

Vocabulary: 1. b 2. a 3. a 4. b 5. b 6. a 7. a 8. b 9. a 10. b

Questions: 1. Mrs. Frankweiler realized that Claudia and Jamie were the missing children because she had been reading about them in the newspapers. 2. Mrs. Frankweiler wanted to meet Claudia and Jamie because she wanted to know the details of their adventure. 3. Claudia had been so busy hiding and then trying to find out about the statue that she had never really thought about home. 4. Mrs. Frankweiler made the bargain that she would give the children one hour of access to the information in her files. Then she would have her chauffeur take them home to Greenwich. 5. The information about the angel was filed under "Bologna," the city in Italy where Mrs. Frankweiler bought the angel. In the file were sketches of the angel signed by Michelangelo. 6. Mrs. Frankweiler wanted to maintain her secret because it made her feel special. 7. Saxonberg was Claudia and Jamie's grandfather. He was being told the story so that he would understand why the drawings were being willed to the Kincaid children.